Lion Heart
Activation Journal

30 Day Journaling Challenge to Build
a Brave & Abundant Mindset

Lani Gelera

Featuring Artwork by Jan Kasparec

All Artwork by Jan Kasparec

Lionheart Publishing

www.fenixfallgirl.com

Author E-mail: lanigelera@hotmail.com

Artwork by Jan Kasparec – JanKasparec.com

Lionheart Activation Journal/Lani Gelera. -- 1st ed.

ISBN: 978-1-7775400-0-5

Dedications

To my Mother, Susan.

May she rest in peace.

Her love, support and guidance for the first decade of my life has engraved upon my soul the values of compassion, integrity, authenticity and courage. These values have guided my journey with loving light and encouragement; reminding me that I am never, for even one second, alone.

I also dedicate this activation journal to every single man that has ever broken my heart and left me to fend for myself in the world, just like my father. Every single best friend forever girlfriend that has betrayed me or walked away when I needed her most. Every single toxic friendship, dysfunctional and abusive relationship I have survived has forged within me the strength and independence to show up in the world with self-love, self-respect, confidence and conviction to stand up for myself, my beliefs and my values.

These are the life skills and personal growth tools, that build a brave and abundant mindset, that I share in this book, with love and courage.

Table of Contents

30 Days of Self-Discovery to Build a Brave & Abundant Mindset 1

Day 1 – Free-Flow Journalling 5

Day 2 – 5-Minute Meditation Practice 7

Day 3 – Holding Space for Yourself 9

Day 4 – Divine Guidance 11

Day 5 – Using Your Clair Senses 15

Day 6 – Attitude of Gratitude 19

Day 7 – Manifestation Process 21

Day 8 – Self-Limiting Beliefs, Blocks & Counter Affirmations 23

Day 9 – Your Highest Version of You 25

Day 10 – Future Vision 27

Day 11 – Goals Setting 29

Day 12 – The To Do List 31

Day 13 – New Habits 33

Day 14 – Core Values 35

Day 15 – Words Matter 39

Day 16 – Social Media Detox 43

Day 17 – Abundant Mindset 45

Day 18 – Soaking Up the Self-Love 47

Day 19 – Sitting with Sadness 49

Day 20 – Facing Fear 51

Day 21 – Warrior's Journey 53

Day 22 – Dark Night Of The Soul 55

Day 23 – Dream Explorer 56

Day 24 – Serendipity 59

Day 25 – Discernment 61

Day 26 – Calling on Courage 63

Day 27 – The Hardest Thing to Do 65

Day 28 – Find Your Tribe 67

Day 29 – Phoenix Rising 69

Day 30 – Lionheart Activated 71

30 Days of Self-Discovery to Build a Brave & Abundant Mindset

So many questions to ask in our current level of consciousness: Have I experienced a spiritual awakening yet? Is my chosen career in alignment with my passion and purpose? Are my intimate relationships feeding and nurturing my soul? Do I really believe in my divine life path and journey? Have I been following my own intuition and higher self-guidance? Do I have the life skills and mindset needed to manifest the life of my dreams? The answer to all of these questions will tell you whether or not you have done the personal growth and spiritual development work that you will need to live the life you came here to manifest.

As we ascend into the higher vibrations and frequency on the planet, we are all being asked to elevate our consciousness, heal our past trauma and consciously forgive in order to cancel out the waves of karmic reverberation we have been riding throughout our life, and lifetimes.

You have attracted this 30-day journalling challenge into your life, in perfect timing and for a reason. This journal will help you develop the skills and tools needed to answer a lot of the questions that you have been asking of the universe for a very long time. The kind of questions that don't get answered in school. If your parents were never taught these skills and tools, then they are unlikely to pass forward this life knowledge to you.

If there is something that you want to know about life, love, relationships, or your passion and purpose, there is an answer for you — if you know where to find it and how to receive it. The universe has a way of answering every single question you have ever pondered throughout your life. All you have to do is learn the language of your higher self-soul and how to listen to the subtle signs of the universe all around you. You already have all the answers you need within you and listening to the universe will help reveal them to you. As you go on this journey, you'll write all the answers to your questions down in this 30-day journalling challenge.

With all the skills and tools that we can learn through personal growth and development, it takes time to contemplate and eventually integrate these lessons into our lives and into our very being. Creating and building an entirely new mindset with new programming takes time; repetition and practice are necessary for applying new principles and ideas. Be patient with yourself.

This journal is meant to guide you by your own core values, intuition and instincts until your new mindset becomes your natural and normal way of thinking. This 30-day journalling challenge is designed to inspire, motivate, empower and encourage you to elevate your own awareness of the life you are manifesting, moving you to a higher frequency and state of consciousness.

Courageously choosing to do internal reflection and personal growth work will help you raise your own vibration with self-love, self-respect and bravery. Writing from your own heart in this journal for even just 10-15 minutes a day will help build up an abundant mindset, empowering you to live the life of your dreams.

When you live in the fullest expression of your authentic being, you will start to believe that you are being guided, supported by your own divine intelligence and higher self. It is a loving and compassionate conversation with yourself.

THE POWER OF JOURNALLING

There is a lot of power and energy in the physical act of writing down your thoughts on paper as opposed to typing them.

You will need a journal or notebook with at least 90 pages available to write in for this journalling challenge, which you can do as many times as you like to reset your values, beliefs and assure yourself that you're in alignment with your chosen path and purpose on your life journey.

Throughout the month, you will embark on a journey of self-discovery where you will learn to:

CONNECT WITH YOURSELF

The first few daily journalling prompts will give you some mindful exercises to help quiet your ego mind, find peace and stillness in your breath, listen to the subtle voice within and allow you to free-flow channel the information and inspiration that comes through you.

- Free Flow Journalling
- 5 Minute Meditation Practice
- Holding Space for Yourself
- Divine Guidance
- Using Your Clair Sense
- Attitude of Gratitude

ASK FOR WHAT YOU WANT

You can have anything you desire in this life, but first, you must learn how to ask for it. This section will give you a number of journalling prompts to help you clarify and visualize your desires, dreams and goals so that you can effectively ask for what you want manifested in your life.

Remember, too, that we don't just get what we ask for in life, we get what we become through our daily habits and the aligned action that we take.

- Manifestation
- Self- Limiting Beliefs
- Highest Version of You
- Future Vision
- Goal Setting
- The To-Do List
- New Habits

MIND YOUR MINDSET

We don't often think about our state of mind or our mindset unless we practice some very specific exercises that help us observe ourselves from an alternative perspective. Our mindset is a reflection of our values and our beliefs, as well as the energies and consciousness that direct how we navigate the world.

- Core Values
- Words Matter
- Social Media Detox
- Abundant Mindset
- Soaking Up the Self Love

FEELING THINGS

Some of us were never taught while we were growing up how to truly feel our emotions or learn how to express ourselves. We are often taught to suppress our sad, angry and fearful emotions and just, "Suck it up or smile and everything will be fine". Our feelings and emotions are how our soul communicates with us and if we suppress and numb those emotions, they will get stored within our body and possibly manifest in all sorts of physical ailments and disease. There is so much that we can learn about ourselves, our relationships and our lives when we courageously allow ourselves to feel and choose to venture out on the Warriors Journey and process our own Dark Night of the Soul.

- Sitting with Sadness
- Facing Fear
- Warriors Journey
- Dark Night of the Soul
- Dream Explorer

COURAGEOUS ALIGNED ACTION

All of these powerful tools and exercises can have a profoundly positive healing and empowering effect on all aspects of your life if used and integrated effectively. Journalling is a powerful tool for communicating with your soul and contemplating your personal growth and development skills. But to be used properly, courageous aligned action is needed when the signs and opportunities present themselves.

- Serendipity
- Discernment
- Calling on Courage
- The Hardest Thing to Do
- Find Your Tribe
- Phoenix Rising
- Lionheart Activated

Free-Flow Journalling

Free-flow journalling/writing is a highly effective tool that opens communication between your conscious, cognitive mind and the unconscious, intuitive mind. Journalling is an inward journey to explore the depths of your authentic soul's passion and purpose. It's a conversation that you whisper to yourself while developing your listening skills at the same time.

Free-flow writing is entirely for your eyes only, to develop your understanding and awareness of self. You won't be graded or judged on what you have written because no one else ever has to see it! Because of this, do not be concerned with spelling, grammar, or how legible your handwriting is. However, in free-flow writing it's best to use complete sentences and avoid bullet-pointing.

What you write does not have to make complete sense or be a perfectly structured sentence when you reread it. The aim of this process is to get in touch with your thoughts, ideas, and feelings, not create a perfect essay. Keep on writing to the end of the three (3) pages. This may mean that you repeat the same sentence several times. Keeping the pen in motion facilitates your flow of ideas.

Free-Flow Journalling is writing whatever comes up and out of you when in a relaxed, calm state. It's also known as Automatic Writing or Channeling.

Journal

Free-flow write at least three pages answering the following questions:

- What are my intentions for this 30-Day Journalling Challenge?

- What higher version of myself do I need to become by the end of this month?

- How does this higher version of myself show up in the world by the end of the month?

- Where do I need to shift my mindset by the end of this month?

- Where do I need to focus most of my energy by the end of this month?

"Go confidently in the direction of your dreams! Live the life you've imagined.
As you simplify your life, the laws of the universe will be simpler."
– Henry David Thoreau

5-Minute Meditation Practice

Developing a mindful meditation practice will greatly assist you in connecting with your own divine intuition, intelligence, creativity and inspiration. Meditation also strengthens the immune system, lowers blood pressure and combats anxiety and depression. A regular practice will help you remain centred and grounded in your everyday life interactions. By taking 5 to 10 minutes to still your mind, focus on your breath and bring your attention inward, you will become ever more sensitive to the subtle notes and messages that are trying to come through you. Quiet your ego mind enough to hear the whispers of your soul and all the various ways that it may communicate with you. The quieter you become, the more you can hear, feel and sense.

Some form of meditation or mindfulness is essential before connecting with your higher self-guidance. You will become very skilled at listening for the messages and guidance for which you have been asking.

Before journalling, try this short 5-minute meditation when you are alone in a quiet space.

1:00 - Sit down in a comfortable position, cross-legged and with your back straight. Close your eyes. Remove any distractions or noises. Start to breathe in through the nose for 4 counts, breathe out through the mouth for 6 counts.

2:00 - Keep taking deep breaths in and out falling into a natural rhythm. Tune into the rise and fall of your body as you feel the air coming into your diaphragm filling you up. Exhale fully in a relaxed state, keeping your spine straight and aligned.

3:00 - Continue the awareness of your deep, in and out breaths. Start to notice the thoughts that float into your awareness like clouds drifting by. Do not attach to these thoughts or interact with them at all, just notice them and focus on your breathing.

4:00 - Continue to breathe and notice your thoughts, remaining relaxed and unreactive. Remind your-self that there is absolutely nothing to do, to think, to fix at this moment. Just be in this now moment.

5:00 - As you are existing in a calm relaxed state within your mind, start to bring your awareness back into your body. Think of what the word "inspiration" means and what it feels like to be inspired. Bring yourself back into the present moment with full conscious awareness of your surroundings. Open your eyes.

Journal

After this short meditation, **free-flow journal about absolutely anything that comes to your mind for at least three (3) pages.** Just relax and keep the pen moving. Allow everything to flow through you and onto the paper. It does not matter what you write, just keep writing until the end of 3 pages. This is an effective tool for allowing your higher self's expression and is also called Automatic Writing or Channeling.

Holding Space for Yourself

When holding space for the important relationships in our lives, we need to allow their emotions to be genuine and authentic — it's okay to vent, scream or cry. The challenge is observing these expressions without any judgement or criticism. These emotions can be very painful and sometimes hard to watch the people we care for express them. We have to allow them to feel their own full spectrum of emotions in order to process, heal and release them. This is such a powerful ability and skill to develop when building meaningful intimate relationships. This is where we allow each other to process our lower vibrations and to heal past trauma.

Holding space for yourself is very much the same ability—and is equally as important a skill—for connecting with our spirit guides, our higher self or the little child within us that needs to feel worthy, loved and valued.

Holding space for yourself means becoming the container of emotions that feels, expresses, processes, grows and heals. Some of the emotions that come up are uncomfortable, painful and difficult to express, but we must allow ourselves to feel them. It takes courage to do something that might cause hurt or pain for ourselves. But this is how we heal and grow stronger and wiser along our life journey.

With courage, compassion and kindness towards yourself, do not run away from your pain or the feelings that make you most uncomfortable. Do not judge or criticize your inner child who is trying to make sense of the world. Allow yourself to cry, feel angry, sad or howl at the moon. Allow yourself to be triggered and process the feelings you have suppressed and held onto. Until you process and release these emotions, until you have the courage to face your shadows, these will stay stored inside you and have an effect on every aspect of your life. They will hinder your healing.

Journal

Free-flow journal for 3 pages about the following:

- If you were your own best friend, how could you hold space for yourself while journalling?

- How can you create a safe place where you can allow yourself vulnerability and authenticity with the intent of healing your energy and moving forward in the direction of your dreams?

- Do you need to schedule time for yourself?

- How can you create a peaceful atmosphere or environment with incense or music?

Divine Guidance

What do you believe about your life? Are you a believer of magic and the mystical forces of nature? Do you believe in aliens, angels or unicorns? Were you raised in a household with religious dogma? And has that helped or hindered you up to this point in your life?

It doesn't matter what you believe in, as long as you believe in something positive that is greater than yourself. You are never alone, and whether you acknowledge it or not, you are always being guided with love and compassion from higher dimensional beings. You are one with the universe and what you believe about your life is the result of listening to your own divine guidance in whatever way you choose to hear it. When you come to understand and believe this truth, you can then work on strengthening the connection with your divine guidance, living the fullest expression of the life you were born to live.

Connecting to your Divine Guidance:

Find a quiet space and practise your 5-Minute Meditation Practice.

At the end of the 5 minutes, imagine a beam of light shooting from your root chakra (base of your spine) down into the core of the earth. Then imagine your crown chakra (top of your head) opening up and a beam of light energy shooting out into the universe.

Call upon whatever guidance or energies you believe in to join you at this time. You can call on your spirit guides, archangels, ascended masters, galactic family, animal spirits, fairies, past loved ones, Jesus, Buddha or the spirit of anyone dead or alive from whom you would like guidance. Just request that only beings with the highest of light, love and intentions for you come in.

Then sit with yourself, your thoughts and the energies you have called. Become aware of your breathing, your body, the energies around your body, sounds, smells, and the emotions that arise.

Distinguish the difference between your negative, judgmental, critical ego mind and the neutral or positive, inspirational loving voice of spirit guides or divine guidance. This will take practise but will become very natural. After a while, you will easily recognize how your guides communicate with you and when you need to ask your ego mind to sit down and be quiet.

When you are finished your session, it is courteous to thank your guides, say farewell and close your crown chakra or keep it open. Stay open minded to the possibility that they are always communicating with you at all times in your life.

You will become a master at tapping into the signs, the awareness, the synchronicities that happen all around you. There are messages in symbols, numbers, patterns, dreams, random conversations you have with others, songs that come on the radio, memories that pop in your head, or smells that remind you of something. Underlying hints and urges will compel you to take action at auspicious times. There are no coincidences in life. Everything happens for a reason.

Here and now, you are learning how to receive divine guidance and develop your own intuition.

This is one of the most powerful tools that you will ever learn in life.

Through you flows the wisdom of the ages, the secrets of the universe and the answer to every single question you will ever have.

Journal

After meditation and connecting to your divine guidance, free-flow journal for 3 pages about this experience and everything that has come up for you because of it.

Make note of every random thought, feeling, emotion, voice, sound, smell or observation that occurs to you, whether it makes sense or not. You are developing the ability to draw inspiration, information and guidance from your own higher self.

"Divine guidance is all around us. We just have to be open and available to acknowledge and receive the deeper meaning and messages in everything."
– Unknown

The Man in the Arena
by Theodore Roosevelt

"It is not the critic who counts;
not the man who points out how
the strong man stumbles,
or where the doer of deeds could
have done them better.
The credit belongs to the man
who is actually in the arena,
whose face is marred by
dust and sweat and blood;
who strives valiantly; who errs,
who comes short again and again,
because there is no effort
without error and shortcoming;
but who does actually
strive to do the deeds;
who knows great enthusiasms,
the great devotions;
who spends himself in a worthy cause;
who at the best knows in the end
the triumph of high achievement,
and who at the worst, if he fails,
at least fails while daring greatly,
so that his place shall never be
with those cold and timid souls
who neither know victory nor defeat."

Using Your Clair Senses

We all have Clair Senses. If you were not taught about these senses growing up, then it's likely that you have learned to ignore them. You can't build a sense of anything if you don't even acknowledge it. We all have natural-born instincts and gut feelings about people, places and things. When we learn about and acknowledge these other intuitive and subtle senses, we can develop and strengthen them, increasing our conscious awareness of the world around us.

"Clair" is a word describing types of clear sensitivity corresponding to our physical and intuitive senses. "Clair" begins words that name our intuitive abilities. There are many Clair senses to develop, but for today, I want to acquaint you with the main four. You have probably used these senses many times but never attached a name to them.

Clairvoyance – The ability to see clearly.

Have you ever been inspired by a vision you have inside your mind? When you close your eyes, can you see events playing out a certain way before they happen? How much of your artistic expression, creativity and insight come from a picture in your mind's eye? We all have the ability to see more than what is in front of us with our eyes. The more you acknowledge this skill and consciously intend to practise and build it, the stronger your sense of Clairvoyance will become.

Clairaudience – The ability to hear clearly.

Have you got an intuitive ability to hear the subtle different tones in music or sing? Do you often hear whispers in the wind, or wake from the sound of an unfamiliar voice? Have you ever been compelled to take action and do something spontaneous because you were listening to a voice within your head? Hearing voices that sound like our own or distinctly sound like someone we know in our head is using our Clairaudience. It would be easy to dismiss this as a random thought or maybe our imagination if it wasn't also accompanied by an intuitive sense that you are being guided and it would be in your best interested to trust that your sense of Clairaudience.

Clairsentience – The ability to feel clearly.

Empathetic people will be familiar with this sense of being able to feel the energetic vibration of others emotions clearly. Can you energetically feel when someone lies to you while saying, "I'm fine"? You can feel a nervousness in your gut when something feels not quite right. Are you sensitive to others and taking care of those in need? Do you feel at peace and content when everything and everyone around you is also feeling the same calm and peace within? This is why Clairsentient people make the best healers and caregivers.

Claircongnizance – The ability to know clearly.

Do you have an unwavering belief system? Do you trust in a higher power within you? Do you believe that everything happens for a reason and that you can learn from every experience along your path? Many Coaches, Spiritual Leaders, Healers and Philosophers have a strong sense of Claircognizance and don't necessarily feel the need to research a lot of facts or statistics in order to believe whatever they believe. They have this sense of inner knowing and faith that they are being guided along their path with purpose. Claircognizance is the ability to just know thigs and trust in that knowingness above all else.

Journal

Write down as many examples of how you may have used the four Clair Senses in the past and not realized or acknowledged your own sensitivity.

The more you acknowledge your Clair senses, the stronger they will become.

Once you are aware of the different ways your intuition and Spirit can speak to you, a door is opened to this powerful guidance, which will assist you in creating a meaningful and magical spiritual journey

"Of all the senses to develop in the world, let those that are common be used by you the most."
– Unknown

Definition of Courage

The word "courage" comes from
the Latin word "cor",
or the French word "la coeur"
which means the heart, or the center.
Courage means to come from the heart.
Whenever we speak from the heart,
act from the heart or stand up and
fight for something that we love and value,
we are being courageous.
Courage is not a physical act;
it is any act that comes from the heart.
Courage is a mindset.
It is a choice that we make in the
face of a perceived social threat or physical danger.
**Courage comes from a tenacious spirit
and a discerning moral compass.**
Courage almost always comes from
the intuitive guidance and instinctual drive to do what is right,
what is just and what is necessary to
move forward and not only survive,
but also, to thrive.
Being courageous,
whether conscious or not,
is an act of love.

Attitude of Gratitude

The more you recognize all the things you are grateful for in your life and express that appreciation, the more you will attract all of those similar vibrations and things to be grateful for.

Gratitude takes practice, just like any other mindset that we want to shift in our lives. It might feel silly to constantly remind yourself to be grateful, but when you do it consistently, you will start to see that grateful feelings come more and more naturally and frequently. The more you acknowledge what you have to be grateful for, the more the universe will present you with these things.

To start building a more grateful mindset and attitude, think of every transaction, tip, gift or kind act of service as an exchange in energy. Practice shifting your focus from the act of giving to the value you receive in return. You can experience more gratitude if you perceive a positive, silver lining in your interactions.

When you get really good with this notion of appreciation and gratitude towards all things, you will see the loving light of abundance and prosperity shine into all the shadowed corners of your life. An attitude of gratitude can shift your entire world view within no time at all.

Journal

Write down 20 things you are grateful for on this day. Go into as much detail about who, what, where and why you are so grateful. The more you speak from the heart in appreciation, the more you will draw these very specific things into your life to appreciate. Write your gratitude statement in the present tense by completing this sentence:

1. Today I am so happy and grateful that ...

"Owing our story and loving ourselves through that
process is the bravest thing we will ever do."
– Brene Brown

Manifestation Process

Manifesting is a natural process of creating our reality and the life around us using the Law of Attraction. Whether it is conscious or subconscious, we are all attracting to us the same vibration of that we emit outward. This universal process works on an energetic thought level, and when we can control our thoughts and energetic output, we can manifest all that our heart desires with ease and flow.

There are 2 types of manifestors in this world. We can accomplish what we want by working hard, pushing, struggling and making things happen. Or we can choose a different way with a completely different mindset. We can choose to manifest from a place of ease and flow. We can choose to call in our desires and enjoy the process of manifesting along the way from a space of humble grace.

Every single thing that we desire in our lives we also deserve, and we can manifest them when we become crystal clear about what we are trying to bring into our lives. The universe will correspond to your vision depending on your clarity. Don't be general, broad or vague. Be crystal clear right down to the emotion you feel when your goal is achieved.

Journal

Write out your #1 goal or vision with excitement, feeling proud as if you have already accomplished it. "I'm so happy and grateful that (my goal) has already happened."

Now, expand your capacity to hold your Clairvoyant vision around having already accomplished your goal and contemplate what is to happen after you have reached your goals. What will be next for you to focus on after you have checked off this goal. Sometimes you are so focused on your goal that it becomes all that you can see in the future. If you don't consider what happens after you have achieved your goal, then our subconscious mind puts a big, scary question mark on the unknown. If your unconscious system feels fear after achieving your goal, it will actually try to prevent you from manifesting further goals to keep you safe. This is commonly known as the "unconscious fear of success". Spend some time considering what your life looks like beyond the vision you are trying to manifest in your life.

If you were already living your vision of having accomplished your goals, what would your life look and feel like? What would be next for you? *Free-flow journal about your vision in the present as if it is happening right now*.

Your ability to imagine your goal and the vision around your goal will help you draw in the next logical aligned action steps. If you create the scenario with positive energy and intention, then the only thing left is for the vision to manifest into your reality.

Self-Limiting Beliefs,
Blocks & Counter Affirmations

The only thing holding us back from everything that we have ever wanted in this life is ourselves. We are always our own worst adversary.

When we have become clear on our desires and what we want to call in to our lives, but things are not manifesting the way we would like, we might be holding ourselves back in some way. It is definitely worth self-reflection and introspection to discover how we are doubting or sabotaging ourselves. Our self-limiting beliefs, insecurities and fears are always unconscious until we choose to face and process them. This is the only way to overcome and learn from them.

Spend some time contemplating this concept with an open and clear mind. You are diving deep into your own psyche and you need to be as honest and authentic as possible. You have to choose to address these issues with your own free will. You have to choose to heal.

Journal

Write out five main self-doubts, self-sabotaging, self-limiting beliefs, insecurities or fears hold you back from accomplishing your goals in life. Write one paragraph per issue and elaborate on why it's holding you back. Write why and when you started feeling this way.

From your current level of consciousness, intellect and maturity, **choose an empowering counter belief and affirmation that overrides this self-limiting thought or belief.**

Example:

Self-limiting Belief: Manifesting a healthy relationship is hard work and takes a lot of personal power. This belief is holding me back because I have convinced myself that I have to do a lot of work on myself before I will ever find a healthy relationship. I started feeling this way in my 20's after putting a lot of time in energy into relationships that did not work out for me.

Affirmation Override: "I now choose to believe that manifesting a healthy relationship is super fun, easy and comes naturally to me. Everything happens in will and in perfect divine timing.

Your Highest Version of You

The highest version of yourself already exists within your own vision, all you have to do is become that vision. It's not about trying to become anyone else, like an idol or a role model. You are capable of becoming your own highest version of yourself when you believe that there is absolutely nothing stopping you from doing so.

The best possible version of you is who you really are on a higher vibrational level. Let go of any notion or idea that is not in alignment with your highest self.

When you are choosing to live your own highest potential in life, you unconsciously give others the inspiration and permission to strive for the best possible version of themselves as well.

Journal

Keeping your goals and core values in mind, free-flow journal your thoughts around the following questions. Don't be afraid to dig deep and use your infinite imagination!

- In order for you to call in your dreams and desires, who do you need to become?
- What version of yourself accomplishes all of your dreams?
- How does this version of you show up for yourself and self-care every day?
- What do you tolerate in your work life and personal life?
- How do you feel about yourself and your relationships?
- What version of yourself would you like the next generation to see?

You don't get what you want in life,
you get what you are choosing to be in life.

Be Bold! Be Brave! Be Your Best Self!

Kašparec 2020

Future Vision

Today is the day that you create your own future vision.

If you don't have a clear vision of your future, then it is more likely that you will make the same choices and call in more of the same life experiences from your past.

Your future vision is not just a picture you have in mind of how you would like to see your life. It is an appeal to your higher self to call in the future that you desire.

Do something today for which your future self will thank you. Create the highest, grandest future vision for yourself that makes you excited about life and propels you to jump out of bed in the morning each and every day. Your future will become what you believe it will.

Journal

After meditating, grounding and holding space for yourself, **practice using your Clairvoyance to imagine 10 different snapshots of the future, 10 years from today.**

Instead of pasting these pictures on a Vision Board, **free-flow journal about each one of them in detail**. A picture is worth 1,000 words so describe each vision in as much detail as you can. (Who, What, Where, When, Why and How).

"Your future will be made up of a beautiful flower garden
full of the seeds you sow with love today."
- Unknown

Goals Setting

It's a lot easier to get to where you want to go in life when you have defined your destination. If you don't clarify your goals, then how will you know when you have achieved them?

Considering what is most important to you, spend some time contemplating what it is that you would like to create for yourself in your life by this time next year.

It is also important to visualize your life on the other side of accomplishing your goals. Sometimes we can focus on our goals so much that we can't see what happens after we achieve them.

The real value of setting goals is not in any reward or checking them off a list, but in the person that we become through the discipline, courage and commitment we have practiced.

Journal

Write out five of your one-year goals by making them S.M.A.R.T.!

Specific - Be as specific as possible with regards to Who, What, Where & Why.

Measurable - How much? How many? How will you know you have achieved your goal?

Attainable - Is this goal realistic, achievable? Really?

Relevant - Is this goal consistent with your core values and chosen life path?

Timely - Can you accomplish this goal within a year, or more, or by a specific date?

Write out your goal with as much clarity and detail as if it has already happened.

Example:

January 2022: I am so happy and grateful that I have already created a successful Courage Coaching business positively impacting 1,000 lives with higher vibrations and consciousness. I have attracted $200,000 a year of passive income.

The To Do List

While **goals** are the big picture of either short-term or long-term achievements, **objectives** are the individual steps taken to achieve the goals. Think of your objectives as a To-Do List for the week or the next day. Each item is something you will check off by the end of week or day. This is an easy way to keep focused on what needs to be done in order for you to feel productive with what you have already accomplished in moving toward your goals.

Oftentimes, we feel like we don't have time to do all the things we would like to do in a day. But if we schedule our activities with a To-Do List or Calendar and stick to our plan, then we really can fit in everything that we prioritize throughout the day.

If we choose to, we can fit in meditating, journalling, exercise and a dog walk all before breakfast every day if we manage our time efficiently. If you don't HAVE time to do all the things you want to, this is where you can MAKE time and make it happen.

Journal

Write out your To-Do List for everything you would like to accomplish by the end of this week that will help you move toward your goals.

You can update this list every week, either in your journal, on your phone or on a calendar, so you can visually see how your week is laid out.

Write out your To-Do List for the very next day to keep you focused on what has to be done. Schedule your activities if needed and choose to utilize your time efficiently. You might like to keep bullet points on your calendar and update it as you check things off to get that little shot of dopamine (the reward drug) that feels so good!

New Habits

In order to attain your objectives and goals, you may have to let go of some unhealthy habits or distractions that prevent you from showing up in the world as your higher self. In order to change your life, you will need to adjust or replace a few of your habits.

It takes 21 days to break an unwanted habit or make a new habit. Three weeks may not sound like a very long time, but you can create powerful habits within 21 days. Motivation is what gets you working toward your dreams, but developing healthy habits is what keeps you going. To change your life, change your habits.

Think about simple habits like:

- getting up earlier at a specific hour
- exercising each morning before you start out
- journalling three pages in the morning or evening every day
- meditating
- listening to podcasts in your car
- going to bed at a certain hour
- being punctual for appointments
- planning every day in advance
- starting with the most important tasks each day
- completing tasks before starting something else

Journal

Write out three habits that hinder your progress and that you will commit to stopping today.

Describe how each habit is holding you back and why it's in your best interest to stop it.

Then write out three new habits to start today that will help you move forward toward your goals and objectives. Explain why you believe these new habits will help you move forward

Core Values

Your Personal Core Values are what you find most important to you in your life. By identifying and prioritizing your core values, they will help guide you make decisions aligned with your soul purpose and path in all areas of your life.

When contemplating your journey of calling in your desires, it is wise to keep your personal core values in mind to help stay on track toward achieving your goals. Without reflecting on your values, it is easy to react to circumstances with careless decisions. This will then hold you back in the long run and distract you from your destination. It's easier to make decisions when you know your values.

This is going to take some self-reflection and inward contemplation. Please do not rush through this step. Maybe take a few moments to breathe, meditate and consult your higher divine guidance. It's important to embrace what is truly important to your soul in this lifetime.

Journal

Start off by writing down 10 core values off the following list that apply to you.

Consider each of your Personal Core Values carefully and rate them from 1-10 based on their importance in your life and how they compared to each other. Then cut your list down to your top five Personal Core Values.

Write the following sentence for yourself (substituting your own Personal Core Values):

"Courage, Compassion, Integrity, Authenticity and Intuition are my PERSONAL CORE VALUES and I embrace these values when making every single important decision in my life."

For each core value that you embrace, write out one example of how and why it is important to you.

"Have the courage to follow your heart and intuition.
They somehow already know what you truly want to become.
Everything else is secondary."
— Steve Jobs

Core Values

List of Values

Accountability	Grace	Self-respect
Achievement	Gratitude	Serenity
Adaptability	Growth	Service
Adventure	Harmony	Simplicity
Altruism	Health	Spirituality
Ambition	Honesty	Sportsmanship
Authenticity	Humour	Stewardship
Balance	Inclusion	Success
Beauty	Independence	Teamwork
Belonging	Initiative	Thrift
Career	Integrity	Time
Caring	Intuition	Tradition
Collaboration	Job security	Travel
Commitment	Joy	Trust
Community	Justice	Truth
Compassion	Kindness	Understanding
Competence	Knowledge	Uniqueness
Confidence	Leadership	Vision
Connection	Learning	Wealth
Contentment	Legacy	Wisdom
Contribution	Leisure	
Cooperation	Love	
Courage	Loyalty	
Creativity	Nature	
Curiosity	Optimism	
Dignity	Patients	
Diversity	Patriotism	
Environment	Peace	
Efficiency	Perseverance	
Equality	Power	
Ethics	Pride	
Excellent	Recognition	
Fairness	Reliability	
Faith	Resourcefulness	
Family	Respect	
Financial stability	Responsibility	
Forgiveness	Risk-Taking	
Friendship	Safety	
Fun	Security	
Future generation	Self-discipline	
Generosity	Self-expression	

"Your beliefs become
your thoughts,
Your thoughts become
your words,
Your words become
your actions,
Your actions become
your habits,
Your habits become
your values,
Your values become
your destiny."

— *Mahatma Gandhi*

Words Matter

ABRACADABRA: It's not just an incantation used by magicians and wizards. The origin of this word comes from an ancient Hebrew invocation meaning "I will create as I speak".

Every single word we use in our everyday conversation with others or ourselves has meaning, an energy behind it. Every word has power. The words we use are casting a spell on our experience. That is why it is called SPELLING when we are creating a word letter by letter. When a word is spoken, it is in fact transmitted into vibrations that bring with it the same energy that propels them. This phenomenon is the crucial step in understanding the creation process that leads to manifestation.

Use More Positive Words

Be conscious of the words you use on a regular basis that might have a negative effect on people, situations and your own understanding of the world. Be aware of the words you use every day and make an effort to bring a new, different energy into your conversation. Positive words have the power to inspire, heal, boost physical and emotional well-being. They can manifest more optimistic outcomes in most situations.

Try using different everyday words that do not carry a negative vibration. Eliminating words like WORRY, EXPENSIVE, AFRAID, HATE from your vocabulary can go a long way toward changing the vibration and energy of your communication with and self.

If you are conscious of the words you are using, you can replace negative words with more optimistic, positive words that hold a higher vibration. These create "spells" or an energy of opportunity and good fortune.

Journal

Write down 10 positive inspirational words from the following list (or from elsewhere) that you would like to start using in your everyday vocabulary.

Use a dictionary to define each word and use it in a sentence. Add these words to your daily vocabulary and see how much the energy shifts around your conversations and world perspective.

Consciously try and catch your common use of low vibrational words and make the conscious effort to cast more positive and abundant spells in your life.

Positive Words

Abundant	Blessed	Darling	Exquisite
Abounding	Bliss	Dazzling	Exuberant
Absorbing	Bold	Delectable	Fabulous
Accomplished	Bountiful	Delicious	Fascinating
Achieving	Bounteous	Delightful	Flattering
Active	Brave	Desirable	Flourishing
Admirable	Bright	Diligent	Forgiveness
Adore	Brilliant	Dimensional	Fortunate
Adorable	Brisk	Discerning	Free
Adventurous	Buoyant	Discover	Generous
Adventuresome	Calm	Divine	Genuine
Admire	Capable	Dreamy	Gifted
Affluent	Captivating	Ducky	Glamorous
Agreeable	Centred	Dynamic	Glorious
Alert	Charming	Eager	Glowing
Aligned	Chakra	Easy	Gorgeous
Alive	Charismatic	Efficient	Graceful
Alluring	Cheerful	Effortless	Gracious
Amazing	Choice	Eloquent	Grand
Ambrosial	Clever	Empowered	Handsome
Appealing	Commendable	Energetic	Harmonious
Applause	Compassion	Enamoring	Healed
Appreciate	Competent	Endless	Healthy
Artistic	Complete	Enhancing	Heavenly
Astounding	Confident	Engaging	Honest
Astute	Connected	Enormous	Humorous
Attentive	Consciousness	Enlightenment	Imaginative
Attractive	Considerate	Enterprising	Impressive
Auspicious	Convenient	Enthralling	Industrious
Authentic	Cool	Enthusiastic	Ingenious
Awake	Copacetic	Enticing	Innovative
Aware	Courageous	Excellent	Inspired
Awesome	Creative	Exceptional	Intelligent
Beaming	Cute	Exciting	Interesting
Beautiful	Daring	Experienced	Intuitive

Invincible

Illumination

Irresistible

Joyous

Judicious

Karma

Keen

Kind

Lavish

Limitless

Lively

Luminous

Luscious

Luxuriant

Magical

Magnificent

Mandala

Mantra

Marvellous

Masterful

Mindfulness

Miraculous

Motivated

Nirvana

Nurturing

Noble

Optimistic

Outstanding

Passionate

Peaceful

Persevering

Persistent

Playful

Plentiful

Positive

Powerful

Precious

Productive

Profound

Prolific

Prosperous

Proud

Purposeful

Qualified

Quantum

Radiant

Rapturous

Remarkable

Resourceful

Respected

Rewarding

Robust

Satisfied

Sensational

Serendipity

Serenity

Skillful

Sonder

Spiritual

Splendid

Stunning

Suave

Successful

Superb

Talented

Tantalizing

Tenacious

Terrific

Thankful

Thriving

Transcendent

Tranquillity

Truthful

Ultimate

Unique

Valiant

Venturous

Vibration

Versatile

Victorious

Vigorous

Vivid

Wealthy

Winning

Wise

Wonderful

Worthy

Youthful

Zeal

Zest

Social Media Detox

When we listen to our higher self-guidance and develop self-love and healthy boundaries, it is important to protect our energy and what we allow to affect us. Our higher-self guides us to unplug from the mass consciousness and systems of beliefs that perpetuate fear, anger, mistrust, despair and loneliness. You get to choose which belief systems to embrace not only in the real world but also online. This means actively cleansing your virtual sphere of influence and removing yourself from energies not in alignment with your core values and chosen path.

There are a number of ways to detox your social media consumption. You can go through all of your social media accounts and delete anyone that you do not know or that shares negative, toxic content not in alignment with your personal core values. Choose not to expose yourself to those that will have a negative effect on your energy.

Delete any apps that you know are only distracting you and wasting your time. They are not productive and they keep you from accomplishing your goals and moving forward. You can choose to let go of all the games that are not in alignment with your own personal core values.

Your personal energy and power is greatly affected by the vibrational content of the information and influences that you have in your online social sphere. Detox your social media and watch how your life transforms into a higher vibration and promotes a higher consciousness and reality every day.

Journal

Free-flow journal about the way your current social media sphere of influence makes you feel.

Are you inspired, empowered, motivated, or encouraged by the content that you take in every day social media? Or do you feel drained, confused, depressed or fearful because of the information you take in on a regular basis?

Write about the kinds of friends, role models, or influences that you would like to follow online and make sure they are in alignment with your personal core values. Choose to remove any friends, influences or apps that are wasting your time or lowering your vibration.

Your self-worth is not measured by the number of likes, comments, shares or follows you get on social media. It never was and it never will be.

Abundant Mindset

If you think of abundance as energy all around us and not just a monetary measure, then you can start to recognize all the abundant areas of your life. We have to allow the energy to flow freely in and out of our lives without blocking that flow with negative lower vibrations like scarcity, greed and resentment. When we are in gratitude and appreciation of all the ways we create abundance in our lives, we draw more of that energy into our experience.

In developing an Abundant Mindset, you will always be provided for in all the ways you need, you will always be taken care of. The universe really does have your back and will provide the resources, the inspiration and the guidance you need to prosper and move in the direction of your dreams.

We can see abundance all around us in the food we are provided, the warmth of clothes and shelter, the beauty of nature, the love and support we get from friends and family. There is an abundance of positive energy in every aspect of our lives and the more we acknowledge our appreciation, the more abundance we create.

Having an Abundant Mindset means that you believe you *are* enough, you *have* enough and you will *always* have enough no matter what. You can have either an abundant mindset or one of scarcity, but you cannot exist in both simultaneously. You get to choose! Catch yourself whenever you speak with a scarcity mindset and choose instead to reframe your thoughts around an Abundant Mindset.

Journal

If you worked hard to earn $1 million dollars within a year, what would you do with that money?

How would you spend, save, or give back to your community?

If you won $1 million dollars in the lottery instead of earning it, what would you do with that money? How would you spend, save, or give back to your community?

Free-flow journal your thoughts about the difference between *earning* and *winning* a large sum of money and your mindset to spending it either way.

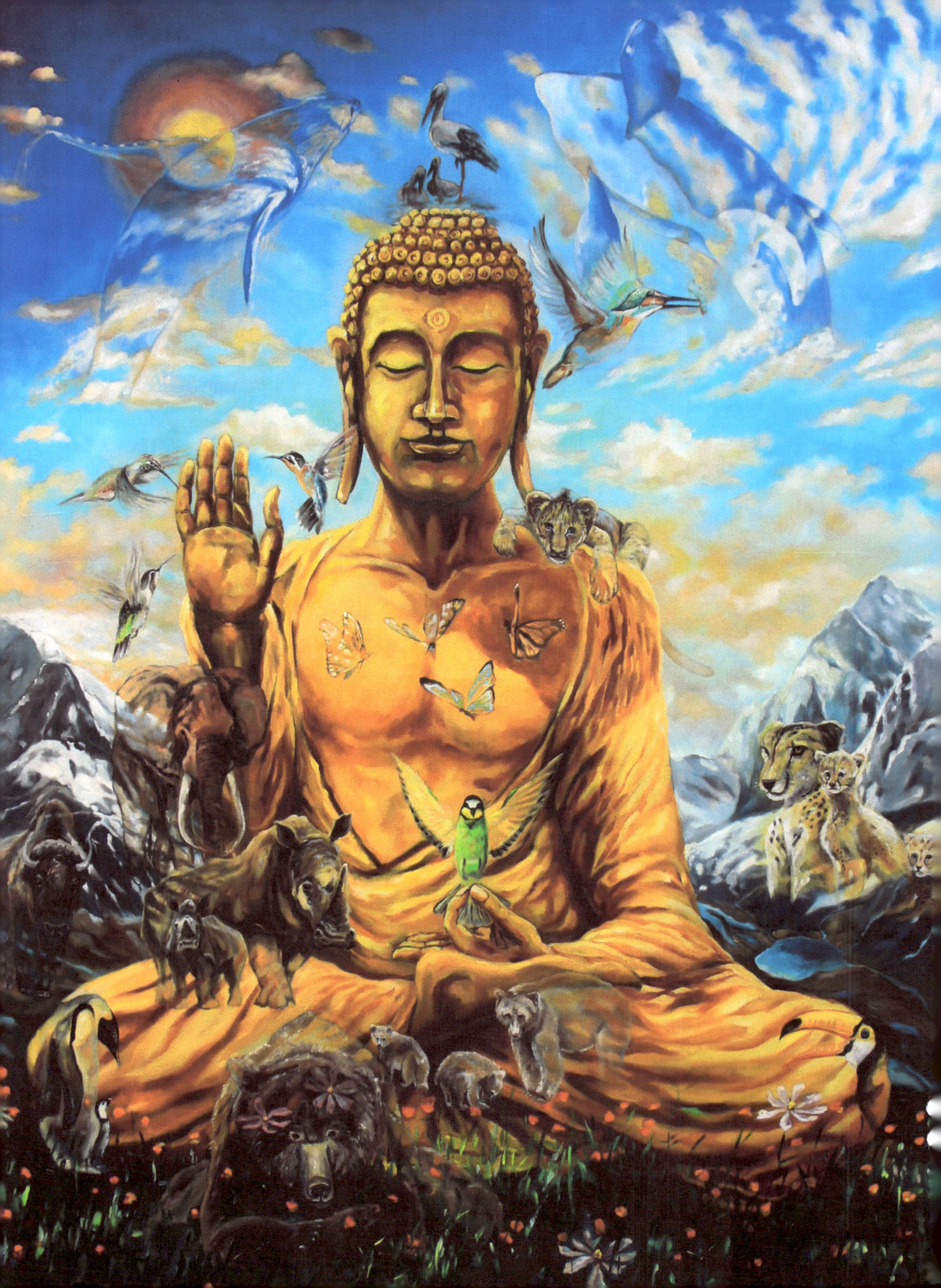

Soaking Up the Self-Love

Unless we are raised in a loving, safe, nurturing family environment and shown healthy examples of taking care of and valuing ourselves, we may not value self-love and self-respect. The concept of self-worth can mistakenly come from value placed on you by others.

Self-love is not something we were or are taught in school, yet it might be the most important life lesson we can learn. Some of us have had to learn about self-love the hard way — through dysfunctional and toxic relationships. Others have spent decades building their own self-worth and self-respect by becoming aware of its affects in every aspect of life.

When you start understanding your own divinity and how powerful you are as a being of light, you will step into your fullest expression of life. Your true nature, your unique gifts, your passion and your purpose on the planet at this time will be revealed through your capacity for self-love. Self-love requires courage and the strength to be your authentic self. Self-love helps you show up in the world with boldness, integrity and an unapologetic rebellion against societal expectations.

Love yourself enough to take the action required for your own happiness, to cut yourself loose from drama and toxic relationships! Love yourself enough to know you deserve all that you desire in this lifetime!

Journal

Write out one hundred things that you absolutely love about who you are and how you show up in the world.

This is not meant to be an easy exercise. Please dig deep, be honest with yourself, be kind and allow self-love to enter in.

This exercise will give you a really good indication of the areas in your life that you might choose to work on, for yourself and with love.

Your task is not to seek for love, but merely to seek and find all the barriers within yourself that you have built against it. ~ Rumi

Sitting with Sadness

When upsetting and unsettling events happen in our life it is easy to fall into the lower vibrations of sadness, loneliness or despair. These emotions do not feel good and can easily spiral into the darkness of depression. Our natural reaction is to immediately try and pick ourselves up, do something to distract our sad thoughts, smile through the pain and have another glass of wine so we don't feel a thing. We are seldom taught the value of sitting with our sadness and allowing ourselves to fully express this emotion in order to heal from it.

You are a perfect, individual divine being of light. In that fullness, you will experience an entire gambit of emotions. That is why you are here, to fully experience your life through ecstasy, love, joy, happiness, sadness, grief, loss and despair.

There is absolutely nothing wrong with you if you are stuck in the lower vibrations for a time. This is a normal part of our life journey. The key to climbing out of that dark hole is allowing the emotion to teach you — about yourself, your experience and your own path in life.

Learning to sit with your own emotions and sadness is a life skill that will help you bounce back out of any dark hole and teach you about your own courage and resilience. *Sitting with your own sadness is a courageous act of self-love and healing*.

Journal

Free-flow journal about a sad experience you have had recently.

Allow yourself to observe the situation with absolutely no self-judgement and note all of the emotions and feelings that come up. What triggered those emotions and why do they make you sad?

If you feel like crying, give yourself permission to do so. Do not suppress anything, let it all out.

Validate your emotions and accept that they came up for a reason. Whatever the reason is, you are allowed to express and process your emotions. When sharing them, be conscious about not projecting those feelings onto others.

Allow yourself to fully feel, express and process your emotions without guilt or judgement of yourself, as if you were a child. With self-love, practise kindness, compassion and support of your inner child's own process.

Facing Fear

We all battle with fear in our life. Fear of failing, looking like a fool, not being loved for who we are, not being good enough or smart enough. Fear is a normal emotion and reaction to a perceived threat. Our fears are meant to keep us safe and bring our attention to a potential danger.

However, instead of avoiding everything we fear, we can choose to face our fears and learn much about who we are. We can even learn our greatest life lessons from facing our fears. What matters is not that we fear, but that we acknowledge, face, learn from and overcome our fears. Our fears will challenge us in the areas we have limited ourselves and teach us what we need to overcome in order to develop courage, strength and character.

We are all forged by the fire. Courage is not the absence of fear, but the mastery of it. Nobody is born without fear. There is so much divine purpose to every single fear you embrace in this life. One way to move past your fears is knowing that you are not alone, and your feelings are valid and part of your life journey.

Journal

Free-flow journal about your greatest fears in life.

Take your time with this and be honest with yourself. Use as much detail as you can to describe and elaborate on your greatest fear. Nobody has to read this but you, so be brave and do the work to process your own fear.

Substitute your own answers to these questions:

- WHAT is your fear? (Failure)

- WHERE do you feel this fear in your body? (Stomach)

- WHY does this scare you? (I will become a failure in life.)

- WHEN did you develop this fear in your life? (When I failed Grade 10 Math class.)

- HOW is this fear holding you back in life? (I'm afraid to strive for anything or believe in myself because I might fail and let myself down again.)

"The fear of facing your fear is harder to overcome than the fear itself." – Dan Jones

Warrior's Journey

We all have our own path in life and we get to choose where that path will lead. When you learn to trust in your path and purpose, you will see that absolutely every experience you have along the way has happened FOR you to learn and not TO you. You are not a victim of circumstances. When you realize this divine truth, you become the victor and your journey becomes that of a warrior.

We all have what it takes to survive through any challenge that we face. No matter how bad things seem in the moment, you are never helpless, the situation is never hopeless and you are never alone in your challenges. The only thing that can ever hold you back in life is your own self-limiting beliefs about what is possible and what you can achieve.

By changing the way, you choose to see your own journey and challenges, you can call upon the strength and courage of your own soul and higher guidance. This will ignite the internal flame of the warrior within you.

The warrior that chooses to trust in their own path and bravely walk out into the wilderness of their own reality does not need to prove others wrong, or insist others join them on their path. Our individual path is our own and we need not justify or validate our Warriors' Journey to anyone.

Journal

Free-flow journal about your Warrior's Journey so far in life and where you would like this path to lead.

What are the major events and challenges that you have navigated through on your journey so far? What have you learned from the life lessons and challenges you have overcome to arrive where you are today?

What are the tools and skills you have developed that will assist you on your Warrior's Journey into the future?

"Warriors are not worriers, and we all have a peaceful warrior within."
— Dan Millman

Dark Night Of The Soul

The Dark Night of the Soul is more than just a bad day or a bad week. It is a prolonged and pervasive stage of darkness and depression in our spiritual awakening where we feel lost. Where we feel an intense emptiness, loneliness and apathy. We are shedding our old self, but our new self hasn't yet formed. The Dark Night of the Soul is a stage in our spiritual awakening, and we might experience more than one of these stages. Each one will result in an ego death of sorts that brings you closer to your own divine higher intelligence and true soul expression.

This stage is when we ask the big questions in life, out into the emptiness, the ether of the universe. The universe will start to answer all of your questions, but you don't yet have the tools and inner resources to understand the universal language yet. All you will find at this stage is more questions to ask. *Who am I? Why are we here? What happens when we die? What is the purpose of life?*

At a very core level, you will sense that there is so much more to your life and your journey than what you have chosen to experience so far. This feeling will draw you closer toward seeking the truth about the nature of your reality and how to find the answers to all your questions.

This is an almost inevitable aspect of any spiritual awakening. It can be more intense and last much longer when we are averse to facing the darkness and shadows within. A dark night of the soul is a phase in our awakening where we are engulfed by our shadow and haven't yet learned how to shine our divine light. We have lost touch with our own divinity and must learn how to reconnect with our inner guidance, wisdom and strength.

Journal

Free-flow journal about your most recent Dark Night of the Soul.

Bring up all the questions that you have ever wanted to ask a divine higher intelligence. Keep asking questions until you write the full three pages.

You don't have to answer any of them but keep asking the hard and introspective questions that you know would change your life if you had the answer to them.

"The Dark Night of the Soul comes just before Revelation."
– Joseph Campbell

Dream Explorer

A person that consciously or lucidly explores their dreamscape is called an oneironaut. The skills that you learn and apply in your dreamworld are very applicable in your conscious reality as well. For example, if you have developed limitless abilities like flying, astral travel, controlling and directing energy, facing your shadows and communicating with other dimensional beings in your dreamscape, this signifies that you are an extremely powerful conscious being of light. You have infinite potential in your waking reality.

Our dreams are a powerful portal for connecting and communicating with our subconscious mind and our higher self-guidance. When we slip off into our dreamscape, it is like we are exploring another dimension with limitless possibilities and infinite knowledge to attain. Our higher self has a number of ways of communicating with our conscious mind — in the dreamscape, most of the messages and information are symbolic and infused with emotional energy.

If we are meant to remember our dreams, there is often a message there for us to find. You can trust that the message can be accessed through the emotions you feel during or after the dream.

Journal

Before you go to bed, make a conscious choice to remember your dreams. Have your journal and pen ready beside your bed.

When you wake up in the morning or the middle of the night, **commit to free-flow journalling for at least three pages about whatever you experienced in your dreamscape.**

Use as much detail as you can: colours, feelings, thoughts, symbols, emotions. If you cannot remember your dream, write about what you were thinking about as you fell asleep. Keep writing until you have three pages.

If you did not dream, try this exercise again the next night until you catch one of your dreams by the tail and can write it down in the pages of your dream journal.

Serendipity

In life, everything happens for a reason, and that reason is not for any of us to judge or decipher. Life is not merely a series of meaningless accidents or coincidences. There are no coincidences and luck is a matter of preparation meeting divine opportunity.

Serendipity is the effect by which one stumbles upon something truly unexpected and wonderful, especially while looking for something else completely unrelated. You don't have to understand why something is happening but if you believe that it is happening for a reason, you will begin to put your trust in faith.

Divine fate favours the faithful.

When you have an aptitude for making desirable discoveries by accident, this phenomenon will happen with increasing frequency in your life. All you have to do is acknowledge the serendipity in your life and you will be blessed with more.

Journal

Think of a time you really wanted something to happen that didn't. Instead, something better happened and helped you move forward on your life path just the same.

Free-flow journal about all the serendipity in your life and how you created those opportunities because you were on your path with purpose.

Continue writing for three pages about all the good luck you have manifested in your life because you choose to believe in serendipity.

Serendipity always rewards the passionate and prepared.

Discernment

The first point of wisdom is to discern what is false. The second is to know what is true. It's not merely knowing the difference between wrong and right but knowing the difference between *right* and alm*ost right*.

Discernment is understanding the deep reason why things happen and the ability to see things for what they really are instead of what you would like them to be. Discernment is more important than ever at this time of your spiritual awakening. If you are unclear or unsure about anything moving forward in your life, then you are leaving yourself and your vibration vulnerable, open to attack or mind control manipulation.

When you are capable of discerning the difference between the truth and a lie, you will become strong in your convictions, having stepped into your own power with confidence and courage.

One of the best ways to practice and develop your skill of discernment is analyzing the information and stimuli that you take in about a situation or experience. Consider this powerful exercise to build confidence in your intuition and gut instincts: peruse the newspapers and discern for yourself the truth from the lies.

Journal

Spend some time in meditation grounding yourself and connecting to your own divine intelligence and guidance.

Grab your local current newspaper and flip to an article. Without feeling the need to research every fact and detail, notice how the article, the information, the words used, and how the energy of the article makes you feel. Take note of the overall tone of the article, the projected purpose of this information being shared and who is sharing this information. What are the underlying intentions and motivations for sharing this information?

Free-flow journal about the way this article makes you feel and if you are inclined to believe every word or if you feel compelled to question the entire narrative. Keep writing about your thoughts to the end of three pages.

"We must learn for ourselves to discern who among us is pure gold, and who is only gold plated."
– Unknown

Calling on Courage

Courage is a mindset that we develop when we are constantly facing our fears and choosing to be brave in the face of a potential threat or danger. Courageous people recognize the courage in others.

Courage is not recklessness, it is being confident and prepared enough to know that if we get hurt or fail, we will have the strength to get back up and go again. If you are going to be brave in any area of your life, you will know failure, yet, you will know how to get back up and stand in your power.

Our fears have a great deal to teach us about who we are and what is important in our lives. In our fears, we quickly find out our values, our beliefs, what is worth fighting for. When we show up in the world and take chances, we call upon our own courage by taking action that is aligned with our heart's desire and goal. We discover our true strength and integrity. Courage comes from our heart and will reveal the true, resilient nature of our soul.

Journal

Free-flow journal about the times you have called upon your courage and done something that scared you. What did you learn from those experiences?

When have you stood up for yourself or something you believe in when confronted by a bully?

When have you walked away from someone or something you wanted because you knew it was not what you needed?

You call on your courage every time you do something you know might hurt or cause you to lose something important. Every time you act from the heart, you are being courageous.

Developing a Courageous Mindset is all about choosing to get back in the saddle after you have been thrown off. Then, finding a way to stay on the horse.

"Being brave doesn't mean you are not afraid; it means you don't let your fear stop you."
– Bethany Hamilton

The Hardest Thing to Do

Sometimes the hardest thing to do in life is something we think we could never do, but we must.

Every single person that has ever done us harm has created bad karma for themselves. At some point, this negativity shows up in their levels of vibration and frequency. This is why they say "karma's a bitch" when you allow the universal law to set things straight.

Whenever you are holding onto hurt, anger, resentment and pain because of someone else's actions, you create a karmic cord of connection that will unconsciously and constantly drain your energy and lower your vibration until you choose to release it. The easiest way to release bad karma, cut those cords of connection and take back your divine personal power is to forgive. Forgive every single person that has ever done you wrong.

When you find the courage and compassion to forgive another, you will understand that none of us are perfect. Those that hurt others are often acting out the hurt and pain they have within themselves and have endured before. We are all just walking each other home in the dark, stumbling over ourselves and searching for others to hold onto.

Forgiving another does not necessarily mean allowing them back into your life or giving them access to hurt you again. You are not forgiving them for their sake, you are doing it for your own. You are courageously taking back your power and using it to propel you forward into a future of your choosing, with self-love and compassion.

Journal

This might be one of the hardest journal entries you'll make here but I promise it will be one of the most empowering and life changing. Please take some time to ground yourself and connect with your divine higher self.

Make a list of everyone that has done you wrong, year by year. Start from as early as you can, up until present day. You don't have to go into the details of what happened but do make note of how their action hurt you and how that pain has affected your life since that day.

After compiling your list, whether it has ten or 100 people, make the conscious choice of forgiving each person with the following affirmation and write it out three times:

"I forgive everyone in my past that I perceive to have done me wrong. I cut all cords of attachment and release them with love knowing that doing so moves me into a higher consciousness, vibration and frequency."

Find Your Tribe

The top five people in your social circle have the most influence on your current level of consciousness, frequency and vibration. Your network = your energy net worth.

Whether it is family by choice, friends by fate or lovers by destiny, your soul tribe will be drawn toward you at some point in your life. You have already agreed to rendezvous in this incarnation for a predetermined purpose and time. The contract has already been signed and you will know when they arrive.

You will find a group of people that will inspire, motivate, challenge and support you and your aspirations. Choose to spend time with those that empower you, lift you up when you are down and make you laugh through your tears and struggles.

Your tribe are the ones that allow you to feel the most you, the most authentic and the most alive just for breathing in the beauty of life. They are the ones that will be there for you when others have walked away. They will come running whenever you howl out to the moon for them. They will believe in you when you doubt yourself and they will be there to hold your hand when you feel most alone in the world. They will know how to hold space for you and you will allow yourself to be vulnerable in their presence.

They are your Soul Tribe and whether they are meant to help you, or for you to help them, you are meant to walk this path with each other, even if it's just for a short while. Whether you call it a network, social circle, a clan, your chosen family, they are your soul tribe. We all need to find our soul tribe at some point in our lives. None of us came here alone.

It is in our relationships that we choose in life that we receive the most love, laughter, wisdom and joy. Choose your Soul Tribe and they will make every day of the journey worthwhile.

Journal

Free-flow journal, evaluating the top five closest relationships with family/friends currently in your life. Assess their alignment with your personal core values.

Are the people that you spend the most time with influencing your mood, your energy and your perspective in life? Do you feel good about yourself and your life when you spend time with certain people? Make some observations on the things that inspire, motivate and empower you in your closest relationships. Do you believe you have found your tribe? Or are you still looking with an open mind and an open heart?

"Find your Soul Tribe and love them hard." – Unknown

Phoenix Rising

Our greatest glory is not found in our highest achievements, but in rising again from the ashes each time we have failed.

The story of the Phoenix Rising is a spiritual analogy of a magnificent, powerful divine creature. Periodically throughout its lifespan, it will purposely sit in a pyre of its own creation. It will remain within the fire and burn away all of the habits, illusions and beliefs about itself that no longer serve it moving forward. The Phoenix will endure the pain of fire for as long as it takes to burn away negative, toxic and destructive patterns. The old version of itself goes up in flames.

At last, when the fire bird is ready, it will rise again from the ashes, a newly improved, more beautiful, more powerful, wiser, more divine version of its higher self. It will rise into the sky and continue on its journey with unlimited potential and perseverance.

Most of us have a story, or two, or three, about overcoming some debilitating depression, a devastating accident, losing a loved one, or the most unimaginable heartbreak of our lives. These are the most impactful stories and have absolutely everything to do with our purpose on the planet and what we are meant to learn in this lifetime.

Telling your own story of the Phoenix Rising within can be incredibly therapeutic for you. It can also be healing and extremely empowering to share this kind of message with others. Your experiences and your lessons in life are your own, but everyone around you can also learn from your courage, your compassion, your self-love and your authenticity.

Journal

Free-flow journal about your life experience of the Phoenix Rising.

Share how you have chosen to overcome adversity in your life and what you learned from doing so. Keep writing for at least three pages but let this be the beginning of your story. Your life has more meaning than you know. **Write about the meaning and the purpose of your life.**

We are never defined by the falls we take in life, but by our ability to rise again from the ashes of destruction and redefine ourselves in alignment with our highest version and vision.

"We can choose to be consumed by the fire within us,
or to let the fire purify us and forge our way forward." – Unknown

Lionheart Activated

Congratulations for accepting the challenge to journal about these spiritual concepts and ideas for a full month. The purpose of this journalling challenge was to inspire and ignite new ideas, new concepts and new possibilities while navigating the emotional roller coaster of your current reality. There is so much more to your life than what you have been taught in school. You are capable of deciding for yourself what you value most in life. You can manifest miracles and you deserve every single thing that you desire. You are wise beyond your own knowing and all of the answers you seek are within you.

This journal is now full of your own experiences, your own lessons and your own current mindset and level of consciousness. This will change as you evolve. Your current level of consciousness is a result of your acknowledgement and awareness of the life lessons and experiences you have journalled about here but you will continue to reach new heights. Though important, this is only a snapshot in time and a glimpse into your life journey so far.

Journal

Free-flow journal about all that you have taken away from this 30-day journalling challenge.

- What were the ideas and concepts that resonated with you?

- What have you learned about yourself the most?

- What are the skills that you will be consciously using moving forward on your journey?

- What was confusing and what was truly enlightening?

- What is your current mindset having activated the abundant and brave Lionheart within?

"When abundant and brave skills are developed, you build an abundant and brave mindset. This is the higher vibrational mindset you need to manifest miracles and live the life you love."
– Lani Gelera

www.ingramcontent.com/pod-product-compliance
Lightning Source LLC
Chambersburg PA
CBHW060807270326
41927CB00003B/83